QUICK & EASY KITCHEN MAKEOVERS

QUICK & EASY KITCHEN MAKEOVERS

30 INSTANT KITCHEN TRANSFORMATIONS

STEWART & SALLY WALTON

HERMES
HOUSE

This edition is published by Hermes House

Hermes House is an imprint of Anness Publishing Ltd
Hermes House, 88–89 Blackfriars Road, London SE1 8HA
tel. 020 7401 2077; fax 020 7633 9499; info@anness.com

A CIP catalogue record for this book is available from the British Library.

Publisher: Joanna Lorenz
Senior editor: Lindsay Porter
Photographer: Graham Rae
Designer: Simon Wilder

Previously published as *Kitchens*

1 3 5 7 9 10 8 6 4 2

CONTENTS

$\mathscr{I}$NTRODUCTION

KITCHENS ARE THE HEART of any home, so why not make yours look like it? You can transform your kitchen without recourse to fitted cabinets and professional designs, but remember — behind every outstanding kitchen is an outstanding decorator, for this is one room in the house where combining fun and function without breaking the bank requires ingenuity, and lots of it.

Look at what the kitchen has to be: work room, family room, storage room, dining room. Achieving all this in a functional, flexible, minimal-maintenance room, and making it a place where people feel good to be, depends on careful planning and lots of clever ideas. The quick-fix ideas and make-overs in this book present some of these ideas, many of which bring a new meaning to the word "recycling". The kitchen is where derelict and discarded objects come into their own — they not only look great but have a useful purpose as well!

The next time you visit the fruit shop collect some fruit boxes — with a lick of paint and a length of ribbon they make great stackable storage boxes. Transform junk-shop bargains such as a window box into

In any kitchen it is essential to be able to find the cutlery, and a decorative cutlery box in a striking modern design is a real asset.

a striking and practical shelf for bottles, or suspend three metal garden sieves on lengths of chain to create a vegetable rack that's brilliant in its practicality, with a quirky minimalism suitable for both country-style and ultra-modern kitchens.

There's also a horticultural solution for the windows. To flood the kitchen with warm, glowing light, yet not with the stares of passers-by, try a wonderful blind made from a length of scrim edged with broad strips of burlap.

Once you've seen how much can be done with so little, your imagination will take over and no object, corner or surface will escape your attention. Your kitchen won't just be a better place to work, but bright and cheerful enough to make your whole day!

KITCHEN SURFACES

Above: Rough-hewn wood panelling is given the lightest of colourwashes, emphasizing the grain without concealing the natural properties of the wood.

AS THE KITCHEN HAS TO BE PRACTICAL, the walls, floors and food-preparation areas set its decorative tone. As a place where food is prepared, surfaces must be functional, but that does not mean compromising on style.

If you yearn for the simple charm of the countryside, this can be evoked with a wash of paint over rough plaster, or alternatively, you could create a classic "gingham" style using paints rather than fabrics. If you long for all things nautical, employ deep azures, petrol blues and brilliant whites on walls to bring the tranquil beauty of the seashore into

Right: The kitchen tile has come of age – clinically white no longer, glazed finishes bring vibrant, translucent colour to walls and worktops. Here, plain tiles were further enhanced with a grape motif stamped in acrylic enamel paints. The paints are durable enough to withstand wiping with a cream cleanser but should not be scrubbed with abrasives.

your home. Today, with the vast improvements and diversity in paint colours and finishes, there is no end to the range of styles available to the home decorator. Minimalist or opulent, industrial or cosily rural, whatever your decision, remember that the choices you make regarding surfaces will have a considerable bearing on the overall mood and character of your kitchen.

Above: Here, floor tiles get the personal treatment with freehand designs painted in metallic enamels.

Left: Tongue-and-groove cladding can be used up to dado (chair) rail height, behind shelves, or to cover a whole wall. A coat of matt white emulsion (latex) evokes the charm of clapboard houses.

KITCHEN FURNITURE

THE FURNITURE IN THE KITCHEN needs to be durable and practical, but apart from these considerations a whole spectrum of interior styles is possible. Storage is, of course, all important – open shelves or an old-fashioned dresser will allow you to keep everything within reach while enabling you to make a feature of collections of china and utensils. If

Above: Wooden shelving can be hung at picture-rail height to provide extra storage. Take a cue from Shaker furniture and provide a row of wooden pegs below for suspending utensils and decorative items.

Right: The traditional wooden dresser is still an important piece of furniture in the kitchen – practical and imposing, it provides a home for all kitchen essentials and becomes a decorative feature in its own right.

you are planning to entertain in the kitchen, a large, sturdy table, which can double as a preparation surface, will ensure the kitchen is truly the heart of the home. Seating can be co-ordinated or mismatched – pull the look together with paint or covers in matching fabrics.

To match rustic walls and flooring, you could distress modern furniture to create a more aged and authentic look. With a range of simple yet effective techniques such as stippling, rag rolling and graining, existing furniture can be integrated seamlessly with your new-look kitchen.

Above: A junk-shop find was transformed with a distressed paint effect, and is now an integral part of the kitchen's design.

Left: This ingenious screen made of chicken-wire in a simple wooden frame fulfils two functions: it separates the dining from the cooking area and provides extra storage as utensils and kitchen cloths are suspended from hooks.

DETAILS AND ACCESSORIES

Above: Vibrant glassware is more than matched by simple woven placemats providing striking focal points that can be altered as the mood suits.

WHILE MANY PEOPLE ARE EAGER to concentrate on extensive, sweeping changes to create a dramatic first impression, the small details impart the personal touch that defines a home. In the kitchen, details bring warmth and a sense of style and intimacy befitting of a room made for hospitality. Imaginative touches to crockery and tableware and creative

Right: Enamel utensils are the perfect partners for the chequerboard effect on the walls.

motifs applied to walls and other surfaces can lift an already impressive design into something truly special.

You could use a beaded jug cover to evoke the rustic flavour of the country parlour or, for a more futuristic look, combine metal and glass decorated with unusual designs that hint at the kitchen of the new millennium. Whatever your plans, great ideas needn't cost great sums of money, yet can make all the difference.

Above: Co-ordinate crockery and table linen for a complete look, or mix and match colours and patterns.

Left: The neutral colours of this collection of jugs provide a note of calm. The jug cover is a contemporary interpretation of a traditional idea; the organic materials of string and wooden beads are perfectly in keeping with a contemporary, natural look.

FLOWERPOT FRIEZE

THIS WITTY FRIEZE HAS A 1950s feel and creates an eye-catching feature above a half-boarded wall. Use scraps of leftover wallpaper or sheets of wrapping paper for the pots, and stamp an exuberant display of flowers around your kitchen.

YOU WILL NEED

matt emulsion (latex) paint:
pale blue and white

household paintbrushes

old cloth

pencil

wallpaper or wrapping paper

scissors

PVA (white) glue

green acrylic paint

fine artist's paintbrush

stamp ink pads in a variety
of colours

large and small daisy-motif
rubber stamps

cotton wool buds (swabs)

scrap paper

one *Paint tongue-and-groove boarding or the lower half of the wall with pale blue emulsion (latex) paint and leave to dry.*

two *Using a dry paintbrush, lightly brush white emulsion over the first colour. For a softer effect, rub the paint in with an old cloth.*

three *To make the frieze, draw flowerpot shapes on to scraps of different wallpapers or wrapping papers and cut them out. Cut scalloped strips of paper and glue one along the top of each flowerpot, using PVA (white) glue.*

four *Glue the flowerpots along the wall, at evenly spaced intervals. Smooth the paper to remove any wrinkles.*

five *Using acrylic paint and a fine paintbrush, paint green stems coming out of each pot. Leave the paint to dry before continuing to print the flowers.*

six *Use coloured ink pads to ink the daisy stamps, using the lighter colours first. To ink the flower centre in a different colour, remove the first colour from the centre using a cotton wool bud (swab), then use a small ink pad to dab on the second colour.*

seven *Test the stamp on a sheet of paper before applying it to the wall.*

CONTINUED OVER ➤

eight *Print the lighter colour flowers on the ends of some of the stems, using large and small daisy stamps. Allow the ink to dry.*

nine KITCHENS *Print the darker flowers on the remaining stems. Allow the flowers to overlap to create full, blossoming pots.*

GINGHAM PAINTED WALL

GINGHAM IS, OF COURSE, the classic country-style fabric to be seen in many kitchens, but here it has been given a fresh new twist by imitating it in paint. The clever but simple technique involves cutting the paint roller in half so that you can paint two stripes at the same time. For a completely different effect, try using the traditional Shaker pattern of brick red checks on a buff background.

YOU WILL NEED

white emulsion (latex) paint

household paintbrush

small foam paint roller (as sold for gloss paint)

masking tape

craft knife

paint-mixing tray

yellow emulsion (latex) paint

small sponge

spirit (carpenter's) level

one *Paint the walls with white emulsion (latex) as a base coat. Remove the paint roller from its handle. Wrap a piece of masking tape around the centre of the foam part of the paint roller.*

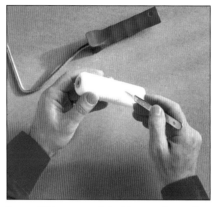

two *Using a craft knife, cut through the foam, using the edges of the masking tape as a guide on either side.*

three *Peel off the masking tape with the foam attached, to leave a space in the middle. Re-assemble the paint roller.*

four *Fill the paint tray with yellow emulsion and run the paint roller through it. Starting as close to the top of the wall as possible, paint even, vertical stripes. Fill in any gaps at the top or bottom with a small sponge. Leave to dry.*

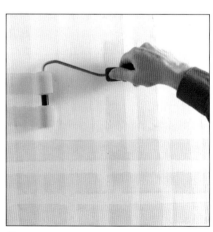

five *Paint the horizontal stripes, using a spirit (carpenter's) level to keep them straight. Focus your eyes on a point ahead and your arm will then naturally follow in a straight line.*

PROVENÇAL KITCHEN

THIS KITCHEN IS A DAZZLING EXAMPLE of contrasting colours – the effect is almost electric. Colours opposite each other in the colour wheel give the most vibrant contrast and you could experiment equally well with a combination of blue and orange or red and green. If, however, these colours are just too vivid, then choose a gentler colour scheme with the same stamped pattern. The kitchen walls were colour-washed to give a mottled background, with the rose motif carried on to the kitchen cupboards.

YOU WILL NEED

emulsion (latex) paint: deep purple and pale yellow

wallpaper paste (made up according to the manufacturer's instructions)

household paintbrush

plumb line

approx. 30 x 30cm/12 x 12in cardboard

pencil

old plates

foam rollers

rosebud- and rose-motif stamps

acrylic paint in red and green

clear matt varnish

varnish brush

one *To make the colourwash, mix one part deep purple emulsion (latex) with one part wallpaper paste and four parts water. Make it up in multiples of six. It is best to make more than you need. Colourwash the walls. If runs occur, just pick them up with the brush and work them into the surrounding wall.*

two *Attach the plumb line at ceiling height, just in from the corner. Hold the cardboard square against the wall so that the string cuts through the top and bottom corners. Mark all four points with a pencil. Continue moving the square and marking points to make a grid pattern.*

CONTINUED OVER ➤

three *Spread some deep purple paint on to a plate and run the roller through it until it is evenly coated. Ink the stamp and print a rosebud on each pencil mark until you have covered the wall.*

four *If you wish to create a dropped-shadow effect, clean the stamp and spread some pale yellow paint onto the plate. Ink the stamp and over-print each rosebud, moving the stamp so that it is slightly off-register.*

five *Continue over-printing the rosebuds, judging by eye the position of the yellow prints.*

six *For cupboard doors, spread some green and red paint onto the plates and run the rollers through them until they are evenly coated. Ink the rose with red and the leaves with green.(If one colour mixes with the other, just wipe it off and re-ink.) Print a rose in the top left-hand corner.*

seven *Print the stamp horizontally and vertically to make a border along the edges of the door panel.*

eight *When you have printed round the whole border, leave the paint to dry. Apply a coat of varnish to protect the surface.*

CUT-ABOVE TILES

IF YOU'D LIKE TO RE-TILE your kitchen but are short of funds, this is the cheapest way of achieving a similar effect: simple photocopies cut into tile shapes, pasted to the wall and then varnished for protection. Find an appropriate motif that will fit neatly into a tile shape. Then you just need enough patience to cut out and paste the copies on to the wall. You could adapt the idea to other areas of the house.

YOU WILL NEED
cutlery motifs
pencil
metal ruler
craft knife
self-healing cutting mat
straight edge
spirit (carpenter's) level
wallpaper paste
pasting brush
clear varnish
varnish brush

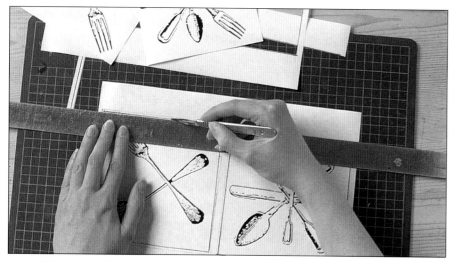

one *Photocopy the motifs as many times as necessary. Draw a tile-shaped outline around the photocopies. Carefully cut the photocopies to the shape and size of a tile using the craft knife and cutting mat.*

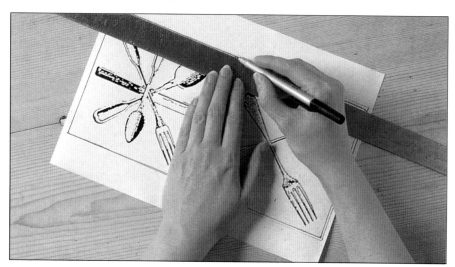

two *Using a straight edge and spirit (carpenter's) level, draw guidelines for positioning the tiles on the wall to make sure you put the photocopies on straight. Paste the photocopies on to the wall, making sure you cover all the guidelines. Allow to dry.*

three *Several coats of varnish will protect the wall and give a wipeable finish. Allow to dry between coats.*

PAINTED BRICK "TILES"

THIN BRICK TILES ARE widely available and take on a new character when painted an interesting colour. You can arrange them in traditional brick-fashion or one above the other. Herringbone and basketweave patterns are also possible. As the right side is rough and the back is smooth, you can also have fun making patterns with the textures. Halved and quartered bricks make interesting borders and more complex variations on whole-brick designs. The colour you paint the bricks is all-important; the same design in white looks very different from ochre, for example.

YOU WILL NEED
straight edge
spirit (carpenter's) level
pencil
thin bricks
brick adhesive
hack-saw
pale yellow emulsion (latex) paint
household paintbrush
grout (optional)

one *Use the straight edge and spirit (carpenter's) level to draw guidelines for the positions of the bricks on the wall. Then, using adhesive and following the brick manufacturer's instructions, stick the bricks in place. Cut some bricks in half or in quarters with the hack-saw. Use the smaller pieces to make a border at dado-rail height.*

two *Give the bricks a first coat of emulsion paint.*

three *If you wish, grout the bricks and then paint over them and grout again. Otherwise, just give the bricks a second coat of paint.*

TUSCAN DOORWAY

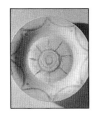

WITH PATIENCE AND A little confidence, you can attempt a simple *trompe-l'oeil* wall decoration to create the atmosphere of a Tuscan country house in your own kitchen. The key to this rustic look is to layer the colours and then rub the layers back to reveal those underneath. The rest of the effect is created by masking off successive areas and finally adding simple, freehand "coach lines", so called because they are similar to the decorative lines on the liveries on horse-drawn coaches. It doesn't matter if your lines aren't perfect; it adds to the look. A final wash of watery ochre enhances the aged look.

YOU WILL NEED

emulsion (latex) paint: cream, yellow, terracotta and green

household and artist's paintbrushes in different sizes

paint roller

paint-mixing tray

pencil

scrap paper

set square or ruler

spirit (carpenter's) level

straight edge

string

masking tape

hand-sander

brown pencil

one *Experiment with colours. You can pick quite strong shades as they will soften when they are sanded back. Apply the cream base coat.*

two *Wash over the base coat with a warm yellow paint.*

three *Draw your design to scale on paper using a set square or ruler.*

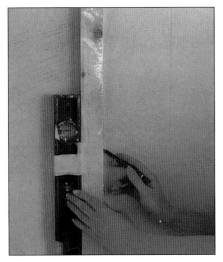

four *Measure and draw the straight lines on the wall, using the spirit (carpenter's) level and straight edge.*

five *Draw the curve, using a pencil tied to a length of string in the same way as you would use a pair of compasses.*

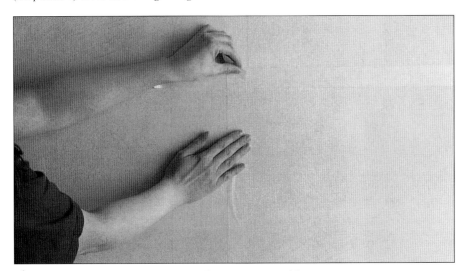

six *Mask off the areas to be painted in terracotta with tape.*

seven *Paint in the terracotta areas and immediately remove the tape.*

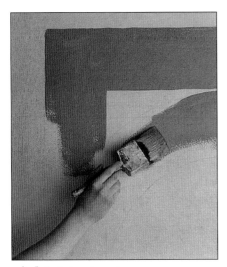

eight *Paint the other areas green, masking off if necessary.*

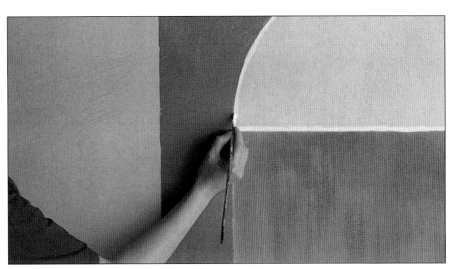

nine *Paint a thin cream outline around all the edges by hand.*

CONTINUED OVER ➤

ten *Lightly sand over the design, going back to the base coat in some areas and leaving others untouched.*

eleven *Wash over everything again with the warm yellow paint. Mask off the squares in the border. Paint the outlines and immediately remove the tape.*

twelve *Paint in all the outlines and immediately remove the tape.*

thirteen *Use the brown pencil to draw in extra-fine lines in the semi-circular "fan-light".*

PUNCHED-TIN WALL

PUNCHED-TIN DESIGNS are surprisingly interesting and effective. They are a standard technique of folk-art interiors, but in this context they are often kept to quite small areas. However, there's no reason why punched tin can't be used over a much larger area, where it will look much more dramatic and exciting. You will need to frame the tin in some way, so it makes sense to put it above a dado (chair) rail; it could be bordered at the top by a picture rail. Another idea would be to enclose it within mouldings to form a series of matching panels on the wall.

YOU WILL NEED

scrap paper

pencil

thin tin sheet

metal file

long metal ruler

chinagraph pencil

metal punch

tack hammer

wood scrap

drill, with metal and masonry bits

spirit (carpenter's) level

straight edge

wallplugs

dome-headed screws

screwdriver

clear varnish or lacquer

varnish brush

one *Design and draw the pattern to scale on paper first. Use a metal file to smooth any rough edges on the metal sheet. Draw the pattern to size on the reverse side of the metal sheet using a chinagraph pencil.*

two *Practise on a spare scrap of metal to get a feel for how hard you need to punch. Punch out the pattern. Put a piece of wood behind the tin to protect your work surface. Drill holes in the corners of the metal sheet.*

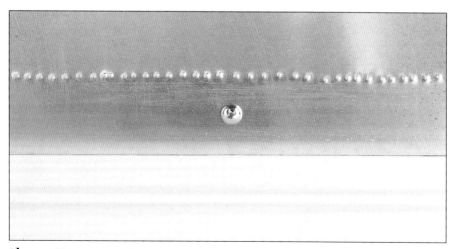

three *Using a spirit (carpenter's) level and straight edge, draw accurate horizontal guidelines on the wall to indicate the position of the metal sheet. Drill holes in the wall where the corners will be. Insert wallplugs in the holes. Screw the metal sheet securely in position on the wall.*

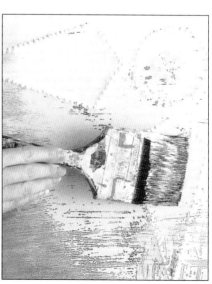

four *Finish with a protective coat of varnish or lacquer.*

COUNTRY WALL SURFACE

TONGUE-AND-GROOVE IS a typical wall treatment in country cottages, larders and pantries, especially when topped with a display shelf for a collection of pretty china. Tongue-and-groove is practical as well as decorative, providing insulation and hiding uneven surfaces. Another advantage is that it is simple to hammer nails into the wood if you want to hang pictures. Most timber merchants and hardware stores sell tongue-and-groove, sometimes even in kit form.

YOU WILL NEED

retractable tape measure

straight edge

spirit (carpenter's) level

three lengths of battening, to fit your wall width

hand drill

wall plugs (plastic anchors)

screwdriver and screws

tongue-and-groove planks, to fit your wall depth – measured from skirting board (baseboard) to picture-rail height

hammer

panel pins (small fine nails)

fine nail punch

shelf brackets, enough to fit your wall width when spaced 60cm (24in) apart

15cm- (6in-) wide shelving plank, to fit your wall width

flat beading (molding), to fit your wall width

saw

white emulsion (latex) paint

household paintbrush

one *Carefully remove any existing skirting board (baseboard), to be replaced later. Using the straight edge and spirit (carpenter's) level, mark the position for three levels of battening at the top, centre and bottom of the wall. Drill and insert the wall plugs (plastic anchors), then screw the battens firmly in place.*

two *Place the first tongue-and-groove plank against the wall and attach to the three battens with panel pins (nails). Check the vertical with the spirit level. Tap panel pins through the inside edge of the "tongue" into the battens.*

three *Using a nail punch, hammer the heads of the panel pins below the surface of the wood.*

four *Drill holes 60cm (24in) apart for the shelf supports so that the shelf will sit at the top of the tongue-and-groove. Screw in place, checking that they are level.*

◄ five *Place the shelving plank on top of the brackets. Drill holes to line up with the brackets, then screw in place from above.*

six *Cut a piece of beading (molding) to fit between each pair of brackets. Tap in place to conceal the raw edges of the tongue-and-groove. Replace the skirting board. Paint the tongue-and-groove and shelf with white emulsion (latex) diluted 50/50 with water.* **►**

TROMPE L'OEIL LINOLEUM

LINOLEUM NOW COMES in many thicknesses, colours and patterns, and while it doesn't quite have the appeal of a beautiful classical floor, by cutting it into "three-dimensional" patterns and playing with slight colour variations you can create quite grand effects. Aside from the fact that lino is hard-wearing, water-resistant and probably one of the least expensive floor coverings, given this dramatic treatment, it can become the centrepiece of any kitchen. Rolls of lino and floor adhesive were used in this project, but you could also use self-glued tiles to make a floor reminiscent of a Venetian palazzo.

YOU WILL NEED

power sander, with fine-grade sandpaper

tape measure

pencil

paper

ruler

long metal ruler or straight edge

hardboard sheet

saw

linoleum rolls in different colours

craft knife

contact floor adhesive

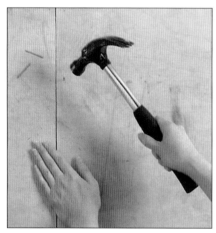

one *You need a smooth, flat surface. If necessary, lay a marine-plywood or hardwood floor. Make sure that no nail heads are exposed, then lightly sand the floor.*

two *Measure the floor. To ensure a good fit, it's very important to work out the pattern on paper first, using the template at the back of the book as a guide.*

three *Draw grid lines on the floor as a guide for laying the lino shapes. Draw each of the pattern shapes on a piece of hardboard and cut them out with a saw.*

four *Cut out the lino around the templates. Accuracy is important.*

five *Try out your pattern in pieces of lino and see if any need trimming. Number them on the back to fit them together more easily. Use contact adhesive to glue the tiles to the floor.*

VERMEER-STYLE MARBLE

YOU MAY BE FACED WITH a hardboard floor and long for the grandeur and impact of a marble one. Marbling is relatively easy to do. A wonderfully strong pattern is used here, taken from Vermeer's Old Master paintings. You may choose to do a simple chequerboard or even behave as if you had a huge slab of marble. Find a small piece of marble as reference (from the great variety of marbles to choose from) to create a realistic effect. This technique is not suitable for anywhere where there is a lot of moisture, but in the right place it can look amazing.

YOU WILL NEED

tape measure

paper

pencil

ruler

black felt-tipped pen

white undercoat paint

paint roller

paint-mixing tray

long straight edge

artist's oil colours: black, light grey, dark grey, and silver

oil-based glaze

household and artist's paintbrushes

lint-free cloth

bird's feather or quill

softening brush

dry cloth

fine artist's brush

black oil-based eggshell paint

white spirit (turpentine)

matt varnish

varnish brush

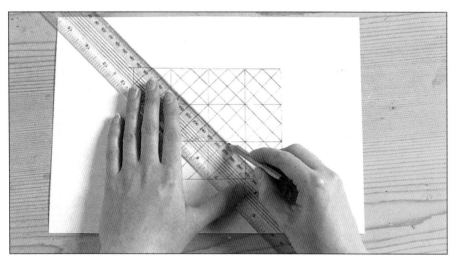

one *Measure your room, then draw a scale plan and a grid on it, using the template at the back of the book as a guide.*

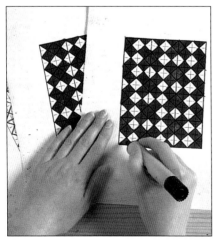

two *Fill in your design, starting from the middle point of the floor plan and working out to the edges.*

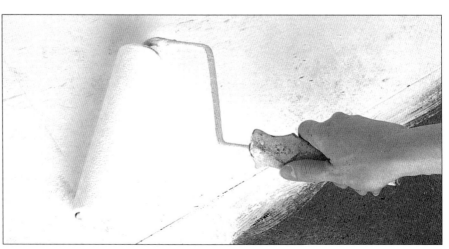

three *You need a very flat surface, such as hardboard or marine-plywood. Undercoat the floor with a couple of coats of white paint.*

four *Draw the design on the floor in pencil. Put a small dab of black paint in each square that is going to be painted black.*

five *Add a little light grey oil paint to the oil-based glaze and apply it very thinly with a brush to all the squares that do not have black dots and will therefore be white "marble".*

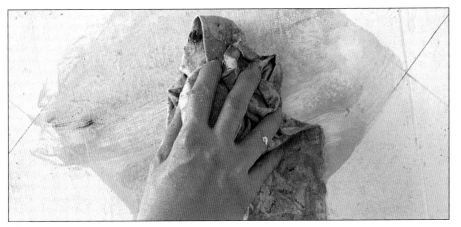

six *With a lint-free cloth, soften the glaze while it is still wet to blend it and remove all traces of brush marks.*

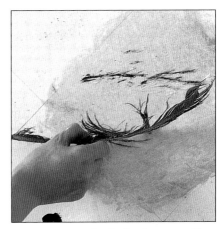

seven *Dip a bird's feather or quill into a mixture of black paint thinned with a little oil-based glaze, and gently draw across the surface, to simulate the veins of the marble.*

eight *Use the softening brush to blur the outlines of the veining and blend them with the background. Wipe the brush regularly on a dry cloth to avoid smudges.*

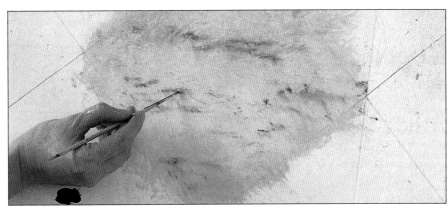

nine *With a fine artist's brush, further soften the effect by adding white spirit, which will dissipate the lines. You can also add more of the same colour or a second colour, but remember to soften it again.*

CONTINUED OVER ➤

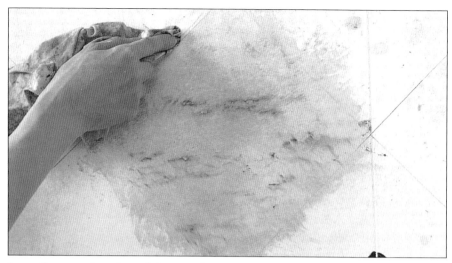

ten *Clean up the edges of the pencil squares with the corner of a dry cloth.*

eleven *Carefully fill in the black squares indicated by the black dots.*

twelve *Using a little dark grey or silver paint, applied directly on to a brush dampened with white spirit, soften the black in swirling motions so that it looks like slate. Finally, give the floor several coats of varnish.*

SHEET-METAL TREAD MATS

SHEET-METAL TREAD PLATES are a versatile and hard-wearing floor covering and will give a room a unique look. They may be painted – either plain or patterned – but also look absolutely dazzling left in their natural state. The sheets come in a wide range of metals, including copper, zinc and stainless steel, and can be cut to size by the shop. Lay the sheets on concrete or a subfloor of hardboard, chipboard or marine-plywood.

YOU WILL NEED

sheet-metal tread mats

wood scrap

metal file

drill, with metal pilot drill bit, and wood drill bit (optional)

wood screws (optional)

screwdriver

floor adhesive (optional)

metal or wooden quadrant beading (molding)

one *Use a metal file to file away any rough edges, but be careful not to create file marks on the visible top surface of the sheets. Use a small piece of wood as a rest and a metal pilot drill bit to drill holes in every corner of the mats and at intervals of 20cm (8in) along all the sides, depending on the size of the sheets.*

two *If you are laying the metal sheets over wooden floor boards, you can screw through the holes in the metal directly into the wood surface with wood screws.*

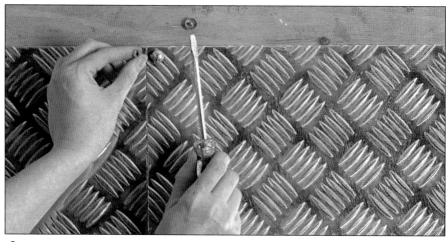

three *Butt up the sheets together and continue screwing them to the floor. If you have a concrete floor, the metal sheets can be glued directly in place. To finish, fit metal or wooden quadrant beading (molding) around the edges.*

STENCILLED HARDBOARD

DAMAGED OR IRREGULAR FLOORS are frequently covered in hardboard and you may feel that this smooth, hard surface is especially in keeping if you have adopted a modernist, minimalist approach to decorating. If you discover hardboard in mint condition, in most instances it is not wise to lift it, as it is probably hiding some horror below. However, with several coats of varnish, hardboard has a natural patina of its own, which is very appealing and works as a neutral background as well as a wooden floor does. Introduce additional interest by using stencils, which here mimic a rather 1950s-style rug, although the brown hardboard would suit different colours. The contrast of black or white works well; choose a bold, non-figurative pattern.

YOU WILL NEED
straight edge

pencil

paper

black water-based paint

household paintbrushes

masking tape

self-healing cutting mat

acetate sheet

craft knife

straight pin

stencil brush

lint-free cloth or fine-grade sandpaper (optional)

eraser

gloss varnish

varnish brush

one *Draw the border motif to the desired size on paper.*

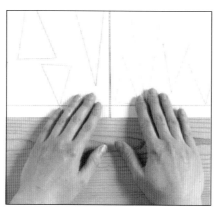

two *Photocopy the design and make sure that the repeat works, by placing several sheets together.*

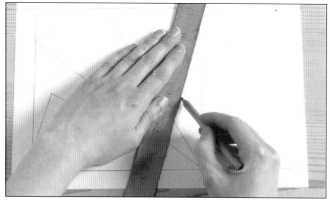

three *Work out a right-angled section for the corners. Make sure it ties in neatly with the repeat on both sides.*

four *Black in the design and photocopy it. Lay the copies around the floor, to ensure that your design will fit pleasingly, and experiment until you have an effect you are happy with.*

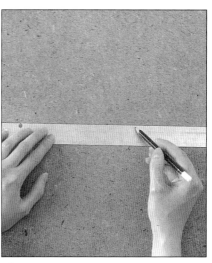

five *With pencil, mark the outer edge of your border on the floor (in the photograph, this is about 13cm (5½in) from the edge of the room).*

six *Draw out pencil guidelines for your border all round the room.*

seven *Stick one of the photocopies, with masking tape, to the cutting mat. Tape the acetate sheet over it.*

eight *Using the steel ruler and holding the knife at an angle, carefully cut out the stencil. To help get neat, sharp corners, make a pin prick just at the corner first; this also helps to prevent you from cutting too far.*

nine *With masking tape, attach the stencil to the hardboard, lining it up carefully with your guidelines.*

ten *Using a stencil brush, stipple in the neat black triangles, making sure that the paint is very dry so that it does not seep under the stencil.*

CONTINUED OVER ➤

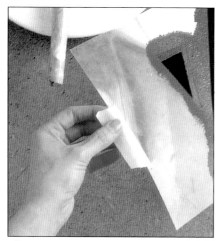

eleven *Lift up the stencil and re-position it for the next section. Remember to make sure the underside of the stencil is clear of paint. If you need to mask certain areas of the stencil so that you continue the repeat when working the corners, do this with a piece of paper held firmly in place with masking tape.*

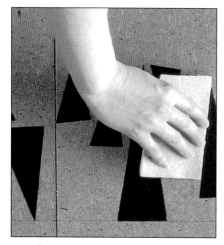

twelve *If you make a mistake or smudge the stencilling, rub it clean with a damp cloth or, if the surface is more porous, very gently sand away the paint when dry. Finally, remove the guidelines with an eraser and seal the floor with at least two coats of varnish.*

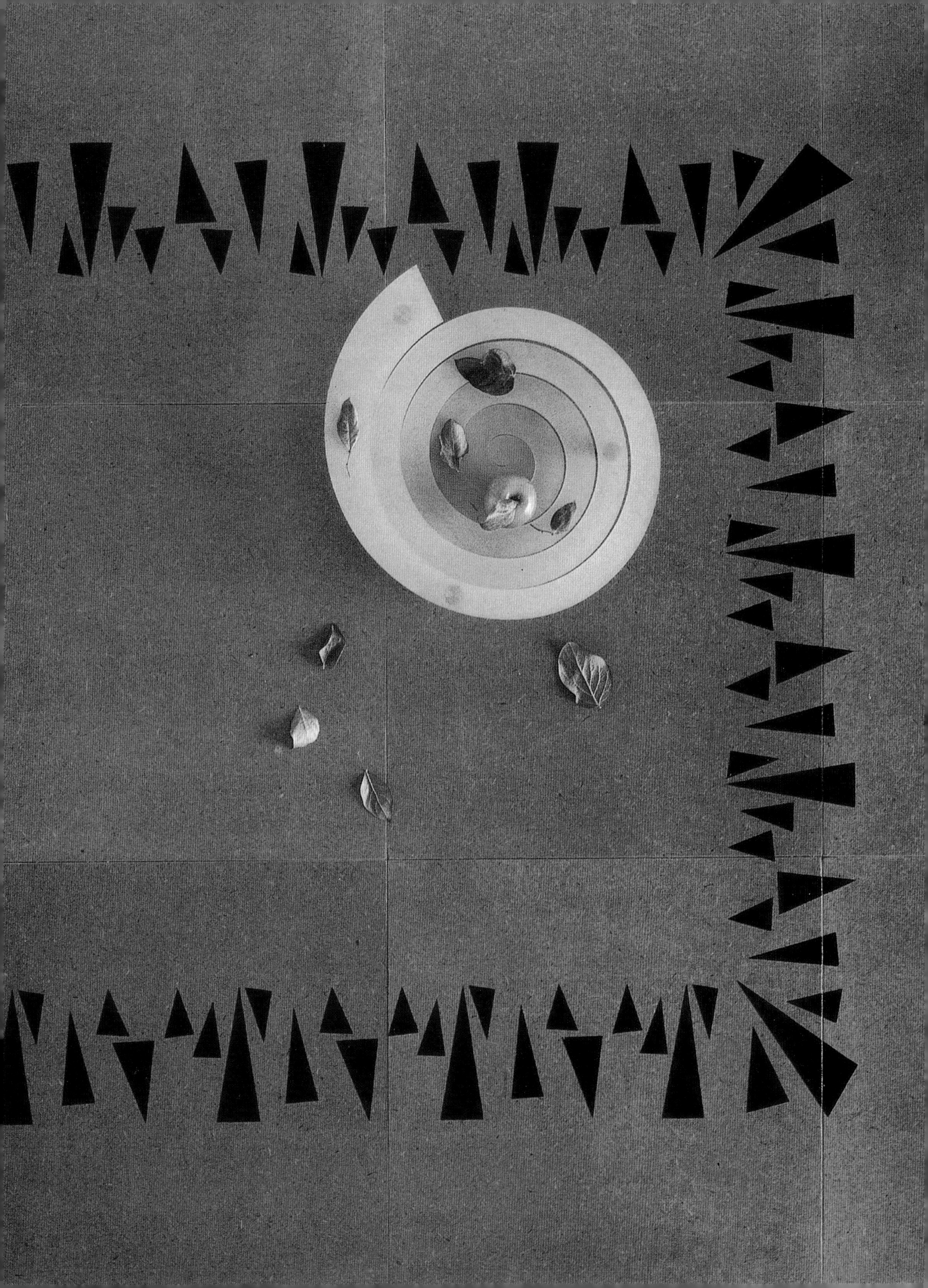

RAINBOWS

THIS REALLY MUST BE THE QUICKEST, cheapest and brightest way to deal with a bare kitchen window. It would also work well in a hall or on a small staircase window. All you need to do is buy an insect blind – those door-length, multi-coloured plastic strips. Then screw two cup hooks into the window frame to hold the rail and get your scissors out for a trim! The one in this project is V-shaped, but zig-zags, rippling waves, or even asymmetrical designs are equally possible.

YOU WILL NEED
ruler
pencil
wooden rail
2 cup hooks
door-size insect blind
scissors

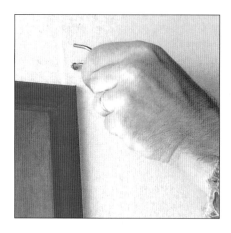

one *Place the rail along the top of the window and position the cup hooks so that the strips will hang over the whole width of the window.*

two *Measure the windowsill to find the mid-point and make a small mark. This is where the blind will touch.*

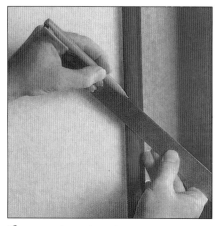

three *Place the ruler on a slant between the mark and the point you want the side drop to reach. Measure and mark the same point on the other side of the window frame.*

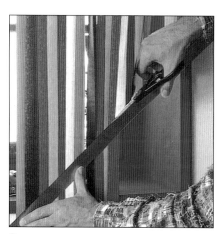

four *Hang the insect blind on the rail and position it on the hooks, then hold the ruler up against it, between the two pencil marks. Cut the strips along the top of the ruler.*

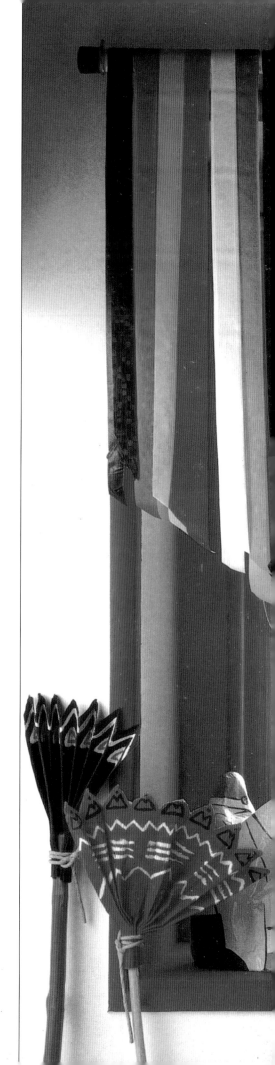

AFRICAN DAYS

KENYAN CLOTHS ARE GORGEOUSLY rich and vibrant. The patterns and colours are bold and brilliant and there is no need to hem, stitch or gather them. Just run a washing line across the window and peg the cloth on to it – use colour co-ordinated clothes pegs and line to pull this easy and exotic window treatment together.

You won't be able to draw this curtain, but keep an extra peg or two handy so you can use them to hold the cloth back and let the sunshine in – even on a rainy day!

YOU WILL NEED
screwdriver
2 cup hooks or eyelets
plastic-coated washing line
multi-coloured plastic pegs (pins)
African cloth panel

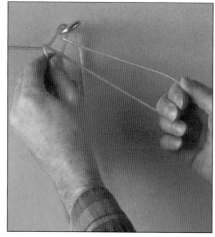

one *Screw the hooks into the wall (or window frame) at an equal distance from the window.*

two *Loop the washing line around the hooks and tie a knot.*

three *Peg the cloth to the line, gathering it up a bit for the first and last pegs to add weight around the edges.*

four *Bundle up the excess line on one side and tie it in a knot. Let this hang down instead of cutting it off.*

APPLIQUÉ WINDOW QUILT

THE IDEA OF A WINDOW "quilt" for the kitchen is practical as well as decorative. It is particularly good in the winter time, as it keeps out draughts at night. The inspiration for this design comes from an old American quilt pattern originally published in Chicago in the 1940s. The sentiment is hospitality, which makes it very welcoming in the kitchen. This quilt is hung very simply from the curtain clips.

YOU WILL NEED

tracing paper and pencil

spray mount adhesive

card (cardboard)

craft knife

cutting mat or large piece of thick card (cardboard)

fine black felt-tipped pen

50cm (½yd) each of cotton fabric in mid-blue, red-brown and olive-green

scissors

dressmaker's pins

pre-washed natural calico, to fit the size of your window frame plus 5cm (2in) all round

needle and matching sewing thread

thin iron-on wadding (batting), the same size as the calico

iron

mid-blue cotton fabric, 7.5cm (3in) larger all around than the calico

curtain clips

one *Draw 2 coffee cups. One should have an outline 1cm (½ in) smaller than the other. Spray lightly with adhesive and stick on to cardboard.*

two *Cut out the shapes, using a craft knife and a cutting mat or large piece of card (cardboard).*

three *Using a felt-tipped pen, draw around the large cup shape on to each fabric colour. Draw about six cups at a time.*

four *Place the smaller shape inside each outline. This will indicate the fold line for the fabric.*

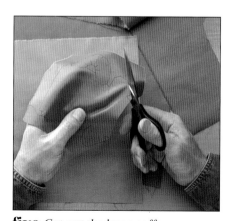

five *Cut out the large coffee cup shapes.*

six *Snip curves up to the fold line.*

seven *Pin the coffee cups to the calico fabric, alternating the colours and spacing them evenly.*

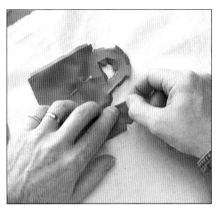

eight *Using your thumbnail to crease the fabric at the fold line, turn under a small hem around each shape.*

nine *Slip stitch around each shape, using the needle to tuck in untidy edges. Bring the needle up through the shape and directly down into the calico, then bring it up further along for the next stitch. Any irregularity is part of its charm.*

ten *Iron the wadding (batting) to the back of the calico, placing a cloth under the iron. Lay the blue backing fabric out flat and centre the quilt right side up on top. Fold the blue fabric over on all sides to make a border. Turn under the raw edges and slip stitch to the edge of the quilt. Attach curtain clips to the top to hang.*

BURLAP & SCRIM BLINDS

THE NATURAL MATERIALS OF burlap and linen scrim are teamed up with bamboo canes to make this unusual Roman blind. The blind obscures the window effectively at night, and by day the sunlight streams through the scrim, making it appear almost transparent. The bamboo canes give the window a "potting shed" effect, and the ingenious pulley adds a quirky touch – not only does it look interesting, but it is also practical.

YOU WILL NEED

burlap, to fit window

scissors

scrim, same size as burlap

stapler

6 bamboo canes

iron-on hem fix (optional)

iron

tape measure

saw

needle and matching sewing thread

12 x 2cm (¾in) brass rings

2 x 2cm (¾in) hinged rings

coat hangers

pliers

pencil

thin cardboard

4 empty wooden cotton reels

4 screws

screwdriver

washers (optional)

string

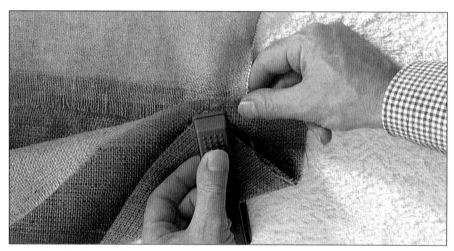

one *Cut the burlap into four strips. Working on the sides first, fold a strip of burlap down the length of either side of the scrim to form a border, and staple the burlap and scrim together.*

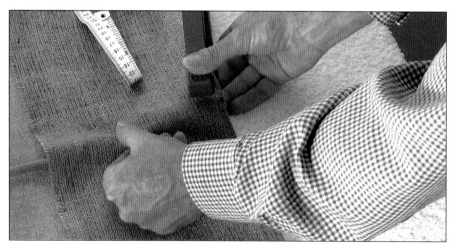

two *Divide the length of the drop by six to calculate the position of the bamboo canes. Saw the bamboo canes to fit the width of the window. Insert the first cane in position by holding it with the ends pushed up into the burlap border and stapling either side of it to make a channel. Repeat this process on the other side. Position the remaining canes in the same way, at equal intervals.*

◄ **three** *Fold the burlap over the scrim at the bottom, as you did with the side, with a bamboo cane along its bottom fold. Staple this in place. Repeat this process with the top edge.*

four *If you are using iron-on hem fix, place it under the seam between the scrim and burlap and press it with a hot iron.* ➤

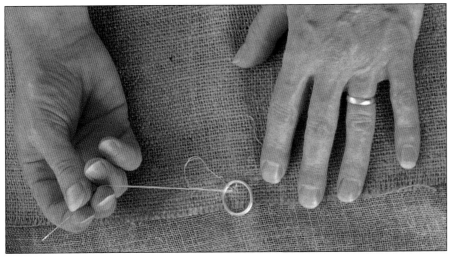

five *Stitch a brass ring to every point at which the burlap and scrim meet on a bamboo strut, including the bottom strut. Take the needle right through the fabric so that the thread goes around the bamboo each time for a strong fixing. Sew the two hinged rings, in line with the others, on either side of the blind top.*

six *Trim off overlapping burlap. If the fabric frays, insert some iron-on hem fix.*

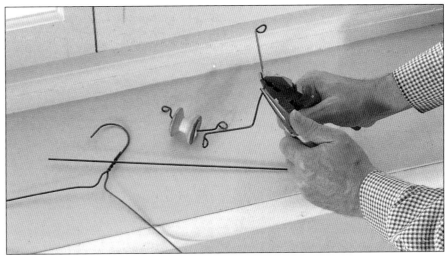

seven *Cut five lengths of coat hanger wire from the longest part of the hanger – three lengths at 16cm (6¼in) and two lengths at 26cm (10in).*

eight *Using the photograph as a guide, draw the shape to hold the reels on to a piece of cardboard. Then bend the shorter pieces of wire to that shape so that they will hold the reels.*

CONTINUED OVER ➤

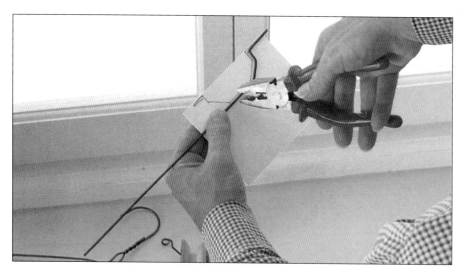

◄ **nine** *Bend the two longer lengths of wire into simple U-shapes to hold the blind, as shown.*

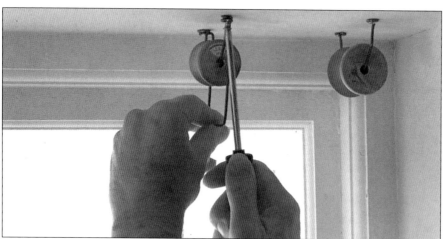

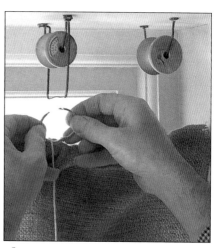

ten *Screw the first reel into the top right corner. Ensure that the screw heads are big enough, or add a washer to get a firm fixing. Align the loops of a pulley and a longer wire and fix both gadgets in place with the same screws. Screw the other reel and wire on the other side of the window, the same distance from the edge.*

eleven *Open out the hinged ring and use it to clip the blind up in position in the window.*

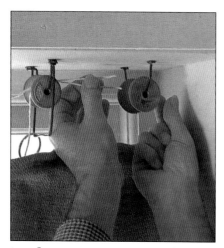

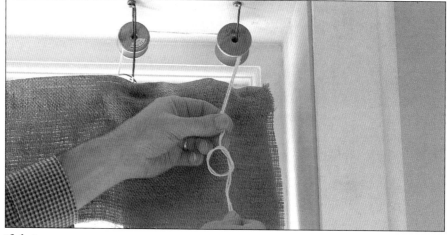

twelve *To thread the blind, start at the bottom and tie the string to the lowest ring. Thread up through the rings and over the pulleys. Do the same for both sets of rings.*

thirteen *Tie the two strings together about 15cm (6in) down from the corner pulley to prevent the blind from pulling up unevenly. Screw the last cotton reel into the wall for tying the string when you pull the blind.*

COUNTRY KITCHEN CHAIR

INTRODUCE PROVENÇAL CHECKS and stripes to the kitchen with soft furnishings; many kitchen chairs have detachable pads or padded seats, and the informality of the kitchen perfectly suits a jumble of frills, ties and prints. Consider the colours and patterns of your tablecloths and then, using bright colours, simple ginghams or stripes, mix and match. As an alternative, smart ticking stripes or pale pastels in sugar-almond colours would give this homely chair a sophisticated air.

YOU WILL NEED

kitchen chair

tissue or pattern-cutting paper

pencil

thin foam

scissors

3m (3yd) of 137cm (54in) fabric

fabric marker

tape measure

ruler or set square

dressmaker's pins

sewing machine

matching sewing thread

iron

ribbons or ties (optional)

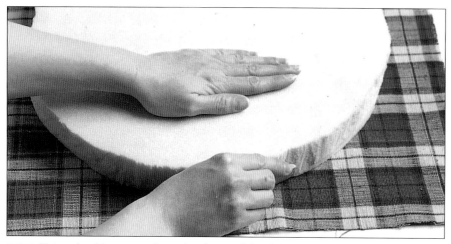

one *Using the thin paper, draw the shape of the chair seat and cut this out of foam to form a cushion. On the wrong side of the fabric, draw the cushion shape again, adding a 2cm (¾in) seam allowance all round. Measure the depth and the circumference of the foam.*

two *Cut a bias strip of fabric to these measurements, with a 4cm (1½in) seam allowance all round. Attach the strip to the seat cover, by pinning and machine stitching the pieces together all around the edge, with right sides together.*

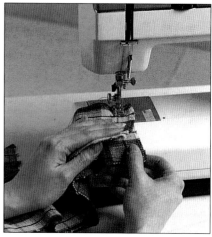

three *Decide how deep you want the skirt to be. The length is three times the circumference of the seat.*

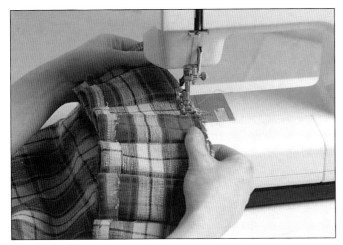

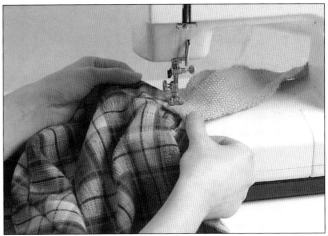

four *From straight-grain fabric, cut one continuous panel or join two together. Hem the bottom edge and the two ends. Fold, pin and press the fabric into box pleats. When pleated, the skirt should be the same length as the sides and front of the cushion pad. Sew along the top edge, to secure the pleats. Attach the pleats to the bias-cut strip of the chair cover, with right sides together. Leave the back edge of the chair cover free of pleats, but turn up the hem allowance on the bias strip.*

five *Stitch ribbons or ties to the unfrilled edge and tie them around the back rest to hold the cover in place. Alternatively, cut ties from leftover fabric. Machine stitch them with right sides together, leaving a small gap. Trim the seam allowances and clip the corners. Turn the ties right-side out through the gap and slip-stitch the gap closed. Attach the self-ties in the same way as the ribbons.*

FOLK-MOTIF CHAIR

OLD KITCHEN CHAIRS ARE functional and comfortable but often very plain. This particular chair was just begging for a make-over and is now the centre of attention. This modular style of decoration allows you to unite a non-matching set of chairs by stamping them with a similar design in the same colours. They will look much more interesting than a new set, and will only have cost a fraction of the price. All you need to do is to cut out the five pattern elements with a scalpel, and you are ready to start redecorating.

YOU WILL NEED

emulsion (latex) paint: light blue-grey, dark blue-grey, red and white

household paintbrushes

ruler and pencil

plate

medium-density sponge shapes

clear matt varnish

varnish brush

one *Paint the chair with two coats of light blue-grey emulsion (latex). Rub back the paint between coats. Mark the centre of the back rest with a ruler.*

two *Spread out the three paint colours evenly on a plate. Pressing a diamond shape into the paint, make a test print, then stamp it in red in the centre of the back rest.*

three *Stamp a white circle on either side of the diamond.*

four *Stamp a dark blue-grey triangle and then a red half moon as shown.*

five *Stamp dark blue-grey diamonds around the edge of the backrest.*

six *Stamp dark squares on the cross bar, then fill in the borders with white.*

seven *Stamp dark blue-grey triangles with the point outwards to make a "sawtooth" border.*

eight *Stamp red circles on the front legs where the lower crossbars meet them. Stamp dark blue-grey triangles above and below the circles, pointing outwards. Add some dark blue-grey and white diamonds to the centres of the lower crossbars. When the paint is dry, give the chair a coat of clear matt varnish to protect the design.* ➤

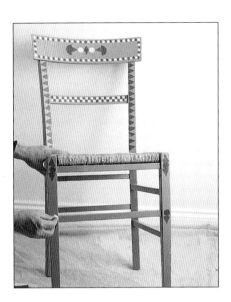

STAR CUPBOARD

THIS ATTRACTIVE LITTLE cupboard fits in the kitchen the moment you have finished it. While its style is individual, it does not scream out for attention, and it has that comfortable, lived in look. It was painted, stamped, then painted again and finally, it was given a coat of antiquing varnish and rubbed back with a cloth in places. It glows from all the attention and took just one afternoon to make. This style of decoration is so simple that you might consider transforming other furniture.

YOU WILL NEED

wooden cupboard

emulsion (latex) paint: olive-green, off-white and vermilion

household paintbrushes

scalpel

sponge

PVA (white) glue

matt varnish and varnish brush

kitchen cloth

one *Paint the cupboard with a coat of olive-green (latex) emulsion. While the paint is drying, use the scalpel to cut the sponge into a star shape.*

two *Pour some off-white emulsion on to a plate. Dip the sponge star into the paint and print stars all over the cupboard. Leave to dry.*

three *Make a mixture of two-thirds vermilion paint and one-third PVA (white) glue and coat the cupboard liberally.*

four *Finish with a coat of tinted varnish, then use a cloth to rub some off each of the stars.*

CHICKEN-WIRE CUPBOARD

CHICKEN WIRE GIVES A RUSTIC look and is very practical in a larder or kitchen. The deep red paintwork is covered with a darker glaze that is combed while it is still wet. Combing is a traditional technique, popular with folk artists and country furniture makers. This style is full of vitality, so be bold and enjoy making patterns. Choose a cupboard with a panelled wooden door. It's easy to tap away any beading (molding) around each panel, then tap around the edge of the panel to free it from the door. For a professional finish, cover the edges of the chicken wire with narrow, flat beading.

YOU WILL NEED

small wooden cupboard with panelled door

medium-grade and fine-grade sandpaper

acrylic paints: deep red, raw umber and ultramarine

medium household paintbrushes

craft knife and cutting mat

firm cardboard

plate

old knife or spatula

PVA (white) glue

antiquing varnish

varnish brush

tape measure

12mm (½in) chicken wire

wire-cutters

small hammer and small staples or staple gun

one *Remove the door panels and then sand over all the woodwork with medium-grade sandpaper.*

two *Sand the cupboard again, using fine-grade sandpaper.*

three *Paint the cupboard inside and out with deep red acrylic paint.*

four *Using a craft knife, cut small V-shaped "teeth" along one edge of the cardboard to make the comb.*

five *Mix a purple-brown, using all three colours. Mix this with the same amount of PVA (white) glue to make a glaze.*

six *Using a separate brush, brush the glaze over the deep red paint. Comb it before the glaze becomes tacky. Wipe the comb clean each time you run it through the glaze.*

seven *The glaze looks milky when wet but will dry clear. When the glaze is dry, apply a coat of antiquing varnish, again using a separate brush.*

eight *Measure each door panel, adding 2.5cm (1in) all round. Cut chicken wire to fit. Trim any awkward edges.*

nine *Using a hammer and staples (or a staple gun), staple the wire to the back of the door. Start by stapling one long side, then one end. Pull the wire taut, then staple the other two sides.*

COUNTRY-STYLE SHELF

CONVEYING A UNIVERSAL MESSAGE, the heart has been featured in folk art for centuries. Here, the motif was used to make a stamp that resembles a four-leafed clover. The smaller heart is a traditional solid shape that fits neatly along the edges of the shelf supports. The background colour was applied in three separate coats and rubbed back slightly between coats; a final lighter colour was applied over the top. When the shelf was dry, it was sanded with medium-grade sandpaper to reveal some of the grain and layers of colour.

YOU WILL NEED

tracing paper

pencil

spray adhesive

high-density foam, such as uhholstery foam

scalpel

deep red emulsion (latex) paint

plate

household paintbrush

one *Trace and transfer the pattern shapes from the template section. Lightly spray the shapes with adhesive and place them on the foam. Cut around the outline of the shapes with a scalpel. Cut out the single heart shape. First cut out the outline, then part the foam and cut all the way through.*

two *Use the stamp as a measuring guide to estimate the number of prints that will fit along the back of the shelf. Mark their position with a pencil. Spread an even coating of deep red paint on a plate.*

three *Make a test print of the clover-leaf stamp on a scrap of paper to ensure that the stamp is not overloaded with paint. Referring to the pencil guidelines, press the stamp into the paint and make the first print on the wood.*

four *Continue until you have completed all of the clover-leaf shapes. Try not to get the finish too even; this is a rustic piece of furniture. Finish off the shelf with a row of small hearts along the support edges, then add one between each large motif.*

WINDOW-BOX SHELF

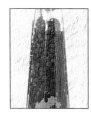

THIS ROUGH-HEWN RUSTIC BOX, stained dark brown, was found in a junk shop, and was probably in a garden shed 30 years ago. It is a good reminder not to write off anything until you have assessed its potential, for here, painted and refurbished, it is both decorative and useful. Hang a window box on your kitchen wall to hold all the colourful bottles and jars that are usually hidden in a cupboard.

YOU WILL NEED

wooden window box

medium sandpaper

emulsion (latex) paint: red, blue, green and white

household paintbrushes

fine-grade wire (steel) wool

button polish

drill, with wood bit

2 wall plugs (plastic anchors) and screws

screwdriver

one *Rub down the wooden surface of the window box with sandpaper. Paint it in bright colours, highlighting different parts in contrasting colours. Leave to dry.*

two *Mix white paint with water in equal parts and apply a coat of this all over the window box. Leave to dry. Rub back the white paint with fine-grade wire (steel) wool so that it just clings to the wood grain and imperfections.*

three *Apply a coat of button polish to protect the surface from stains and to improve the aged effect. Drill two holes in the back of the window box and attach it to the kitchen wall.*

ON THE SHELF

EVERYONE HAS SHELVES somewhere in the home, but how many of us have thought of dressing them with different styles of edging? This project includes three different designs using natural materials that would be suitable for a kitchen. Experiment with anything and everything around the home, and you'll be surprised at just how innovative and exciting shelf edging can be. If you fix your trimmings with double-sided tape, they can be removed in an instant so, with very little effort, you can change the designs as often as you like.

YOU WILL NEED

tape measure

string

scissors

sticky tape

red raffia

Chinese-language newspaper

pencil

double-sided tape or drawing pins

one *Measure the length of your shelf. Cut a piece of string about 5cm (2in) longer than the shelf, so it can turn around the corners. Cut more lengths of string, approximately 15–20cm (6–8in) long.*

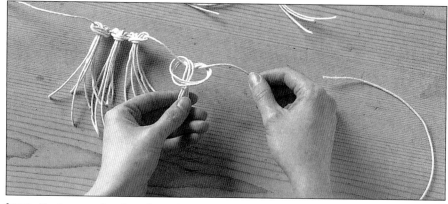

two *Gather together bunches of about three lengths of string. Fold the bunches into loops and then pass the ends over the string and through the centre of the loop. Pull the loops taut to secure them. You can tape the string to the work surface if it makes it easier to work on it. Cut small pieces of red raffia and tie them into small knots between every two or three strands of looped string. Cut the raffia close to the knot.*

three *For the newspaper edging, measure the shelf. Cut strips the length of the shelf, and the depth you require. Fold each strip, concertina-fashion.*

four *Experiment by drawing different designs on to each folded strip. Cut out the edging shapes. Open them out and smooth them flat. Choose the shape that co-ordinates best with the style of decoration in the kitchen or reflects the shapes of the contents of the shelves.*

five *For the raffia edging, cut a piece of raffia the length of the shelf. Cut many short lengths of raffia.*

six *Loop them singly on to the main piece, as for the string edging. Tighten the loops and fill in any gaps. Trim the ends to one length to make an even fringe. Use double-sided tape or drawing pins to attach the trimmings to the edge of each shelf.*

HANGING JAM JARS

THIS BRIGHT IDEA FOR getting double mileage out of kitchen shelves is borrowed from a tool shed. Woodworkers and gardeners line the undersides of their shelves with jam jar lids and then screw in jars filled with nuts, bolts, nails, screws and other useful things. Everything is kept tidy, on view and within easy reach. Fill your jars with cookies, rice or different types of beans and lentils. You could even use smaller jars to create an unusual and inexpensive herb and spice rack.

YOU WILL NEED

4 or more jam jars, with lids

kitchen shelf

pencil

bradawl

screws (no longer than the shelf depth)

screwdriver

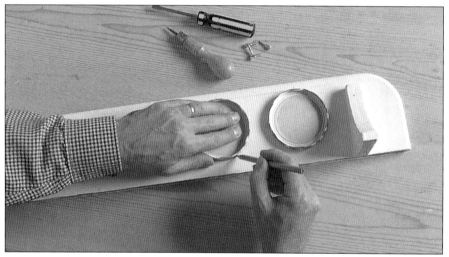

one *Arrange the jam jar lids along the underside of the shelf. There should be sufficient room between them for a hand to fit and sufficient depth for the jars to fit. Lightly mark the positions with a pencil.*

two *Use a bradawl to make two holes through each lid into the shelf.*

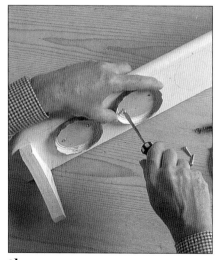

three *Screw the lids securely in place.*

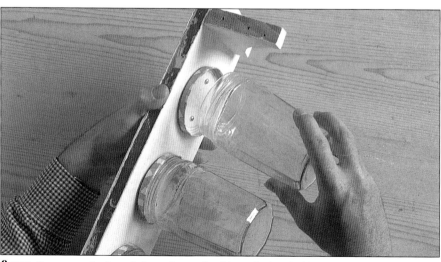

four *Screw on the jars. It is easier to do this with the shelf on a work surface than with the shelf already hanging on the wall. Hang up the shelf.*

TRELLIS HANGING RACK

A GARDEN TRELLIS MAKES AN effective hanging rack. Extend the trellis to make regular diamond shapes and then frame it with wood to give a finished look. You could confine this idea to a small area or join a few pieces of trellis together to run the whole length of a wall. Put hooks on as many crossovers as you want, and collect decorative items, as well as the more mundane utilitarian objects, to make part of the display. Move things from time to time, so the display always offers something new to catch the eye.

YOU WILL NEED
tape measure

pencil

length of garden trellis

hack-saw

2.5 x 2.5cm (1 x 1in) wood lengths

mitre block and saw or mitre saw

dowel length

wood screws

screwdriver

drill, with wood, metal and masonry bits

burnt-orange emulsion (latex) paint

household paintbrush

wall plugs (plastic anchors)

wood filler

one *Measure the area you want to cover and mark out the area on the trellis. Cut the trellis to size with a hack-saw. Measure and cut the lengths of wood to make the frame. Mitre the corners using a mitre block or mitre saw. Screw the frame together.*

two *Mark the dowel into lengths and cut a notch in each length, for hanging hooks. Cut the dowel into lengths, using the mitre block or mitre saw.*

three *If the trellis is riveted at the crossovers, drill out the rivets. Position the dowel pegs on the trellis over the crossovers. Screw the pegs to the trellis. Paint the trellis and the frame with emulsion (latex) paint in your chosen colour. Burnt-orange has been used here.*

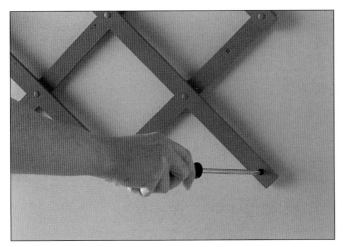

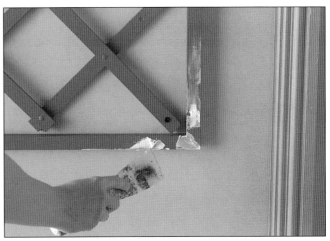

four *Drill holes in the wall with a masonry bit and insert wall plugs. Drill pilot holes in the trellis slightly smaller than the screws, to stop the wood from splitting, and then screw the trellis to the wall.*

five *Fix the frame around the trellis by screwing it on to the wall. Fill and paint over the tops of the screws and any gaps. When the trellis and frame are dry, give the whole hanging rack a second coat of paint.*

VEGETABLE RACK

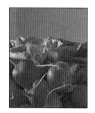

MOST KITCHEN ACCESSORIES seem to be made from practical but unattractive plastic, or high-tech and expensive chrome or stainless steel. This smart black vegetable rack is not the product of a design team from Tokyo, Milan or Paris – although it looks as if it could be – but is, in fact, three garden sieves (made either from wood and wire or galvanized iron) and a length of gatepost chain! Vegetables look enticing on display in a shop so why not store them in a place where they can be seen and appreciated? Suspend this rack in a kitchen corner so you can reach the vegetables easily when you need them for cooking.

YOU WILL NEED

3m (3yd) chain, plus length to hang the rack from the ceiling

hack-saw

pliers

string

3 metal garden sieves

felt-tipped marker pen

scissors

masking tape

kitchen cloth

centre punch

hammer

drill, with metal and wood bits

15 "S" hooks (optional)

combine hook

ceiling hook and fixings
(or long wall bracket)

one *Saw the chain into nine sets of twelve links, only sawing through one half of each link. Prise the links apart with pliers to separate the nine sections.*

two *Wrap a piece of string around one of the sieves to measure the circumference. Mark the measurement on the string. Cut the string to length.*

three *Fold the string into three equal lengths, marking it with the felt-tipped pen as you do so.*

four *Place the marked string around one of the sieves and stick masking tape on each third around the edge. The other two sieves need six marks – three around the top edge and three around the base edge. It is important to do this accurately so that the rack hangs level.*

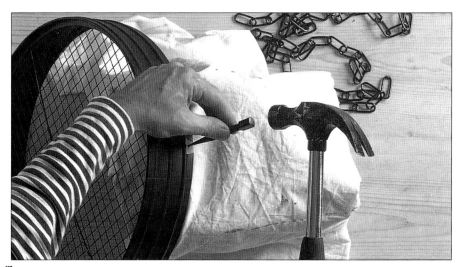

five *Place the sieves on a hard surface covered by a kitchen cloth. Use a centre punch with a hammer to dent the metal at each marked point.*

six *Using the dent marks as guides, drill holes on all three sieves. The dent mark should prevent the drill bit from slipping on the metal.*

seven *Insert "S" hooks into all the holes. Arrange the sieves in the order in which they will hang – the sieve with only three drilled holes goes on the bottom tier. Starting with the three-holed sieve, attach a length of chain to each "S" hook, adjusting the level to suit your needs by attaching the hooks at different links. To save expense, you could dispense with the "S" hooks and simply prise apart and then rejoin the chain links to attach the sieves directly.*

CONTINUED OVER ➤

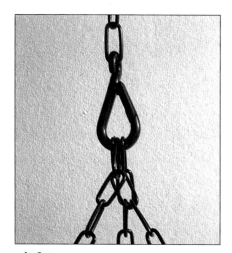

eight *Clip the three top chain lengths together with a combine hook and add a further length of chain to suspend the rack from the ceiling. Find a beam for the ceiling hook as it needs to be strong to support the weight of vegetables.*

Above: The vegetable rack will look equally at home in a rustic interior or a stark, modern one.

Mediterranean Crates

WOODEN FRUIT AND VEGETABLE crates are much too good to be thrown away once their original contents have been used up, so rescue them from your local greengrocer and dress them up with colour and ribbon to make a great set of useful containers. The crates here work especially well, as they have a solid base that can be separated and used as a lid. These rustic Mediterranean crates look wonderful stacked with candles, tablecloths or other bright bits and pieces.

YOU WILL NEED

3 wooden fruit or vegetable crates

medium-grade sandpaper

pliers

wire cutters

staple gun (optional)

powder paint: red, blue and green

household paintbrushes

100cm (40in) checked ribbon

scissors

one *Rub off any rough edges on the crates with sandpaper. Detach the base from one of them to be the "lid". Remove and replace any protruding staples if necessary.*

two *Mix the powder paints according to the manufacturer's instructions. Paint one of the crates red on the inside, blue on the outside, and green along the top edges.*

three *Paint the other crate green on the inside, blue on the outside, and red along the top edges.*

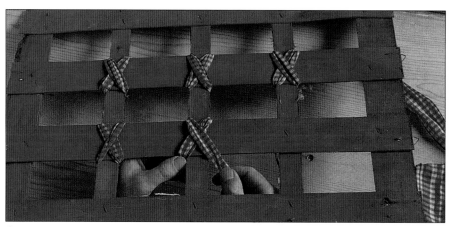

four *Paint the lid blue. Bind the six centre joints with crosses of checked ribbon, tied securely at the back.*

CUTLERY BOX

THIS PROJECT FUSES THE clarity of high-tech design with the starkness of surrealist sculpture – and it provides an ideal place to keep your cutlery at the same time! The stylish boxes look especially good in a modern kitchen, where chrome and stainless steel keep the lines crisp and the surfaces reflective. Make separate boxes for knives, forks and spoons and say goodbye to rummaging in the kitchen drawer.

YOU WILL NEED

small silver-plated knife, fork and spoon, polished

3 metal boxes with lids

felt-tipped marker pen

coarse-grade sandpaper

metal file

metal-bonding compound (Chemical Metal)

craft knife

one *Bend the knife to a right angle halfway along the handle, over the edge of a table if necessary. Mark the position of the knife on the box. Roughen the parts of the knife and the box that will touch, with sandpaper and a file respectively.*

two *Mix the metal-bonding compound. Follow the manufacturer's instructions. Apply to the roughened area on the lid. The knife is fixed at this point, so the bond must be strong.*

three *Press the knife handle into position on the bonding. Use a fine instrument, such as a craft knife, to remove any excess bonding. Repeat these steps for the fork and spoon and their two metal boxes.*

TACTILE TABLECLOTH

ALL SORTS OF WONDERFUL ribbon, trimmings and edgings are now available, and a trip around a fabric department can, with a little imagination, generate any number of ideas. Here, simple upholsterer's webbing was used to edge a plain and practical burlap cloth. The webbing was decorated with string in very loose loops. The charm of this simple design lies in its interesting textures, so it is probably best to use materials in shades of the same colours, as here. However, if you wish, you could make a bold statement in bright primaries or a combination of contrasting colours.

YOU WILL NEED

about 2½m (2½yd) burlap

scissors

dressmaker's pins

needle and tacking (basting) thread

iron

sewing machine

matching sewing thread

8½m (8½yd) webbing

brown string

one *Cut the burlap to the size required, allowing for hems. Turn under the hems and pin, tack (baste), press and machine-stitch. Cut a length of webbing to go around all four sides. Pin and machine-stitch the webbing around the edge.*

two *Lay the string on the length of webbing and twist to experiment with different designs – a repeating pattern will look more professional.*

three *Pin, tack and hand-stitch the string to the webbing, to hold it securely. It doesn't matter if there are gaps in the stitching; the looseness of the string is all part of the effect.*

PURE PLASTIC

A PLASTIC TABLECLOTH is invaluable on a table that gets a lot of use – in a family breakfast room for example – as it can be wiped clean in seconds and doesn't stain. As a rule, however, ready-made plastic cloths tend to be very plain or extremely garish. To make an attractive as well as practical cloth, why not cut a shaped trim from white plastic and make a simple design along the edge using a hole punch? Inexpensive, quick and easy to make – what could be better?

YOU WILL NEED

tape measure

plastic fabric

dressmaker's scissors

pencil

cardboard

scissors

hole punch

ribbon, string or rope
(optional)

one *Measure your table and cut the plastic fabric to the required size. Draw up and cut out a cardboard template for the scalloped edge. Draw lightly around the template on the wrong side of the plastic fabric with a pencil.*

two *Cut the edging shape with sharp dressmaker's scissors, keeping the scallops rounded and even.*

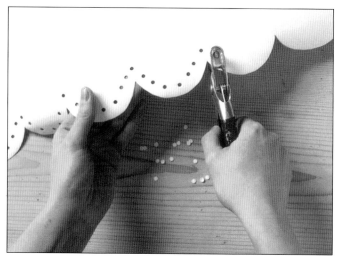

three *Punch out a design with a hole punch. You could thread ribbon, string or rope through the holes to add even more interest, and, perhaps, a splash of colour.*

CLOVER-LEAF TABLECLOTH

THIS FRESH FOUR-LEAF CLOVER pattern is done very simply with a potato print. The cut potato exudes a starchy liquid that blends into the ink and adds translucence. The best fabric to print on is 100% cotton, pre-washed to remove any glaze or stiffener. The result should look hand-printed, so don't despair if the edge of the potato picks up colour and prints it occasionally – it will add energy and life to the pattern. If you take a short break, place the potato in iced water and dry with kitchen paper (paper towel).

YOU WILL NEED

old blanket

drawing pins (thumb tacks)

medium-size fresh potato

sharp knife and cutting board

small artist's paintbrush

leaf green water-based block printing fabric ink (or standard colours: green, blue and red)

craft knife

sharp kitchen knife

sheet of glass

palette knife

small gloss paint roller

white 100% cotton fabric, pre-washed and ironed, to fit your table

sewing machine or needle and matching sewing thread

cotton fabric for napkins

one *Pin the blanket to the tabletop, using drawing pins (thumb tacks) – this allows some "give" when you apply pressure. Cut through the potato in one smooth movement to give a flat surface.*

two *Practise painting the clover leaf on paper, copying the pattern freehand. When you are confident, paint the shape on the potato.*

three *Cut carefully around the shape, using a craft knife. Use smooth, flowing movements to avoid jagged edges. Cut around the internal shapes. Scoop out the potato flesh with the end of the knife blade.*

four *Cut away the waste potato to a depth of about 6mm (¼in).*

five *Using a kitchen knife, trim the potato into a square. Cut a groove all around, about halfway down – this will make it easier to hold.*

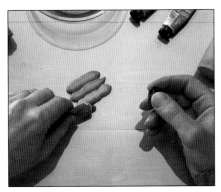

six *If you are using standard colours, mix 2 parts green, 1 part blue, ¼ part red, or use ready-mixed leaf green.*

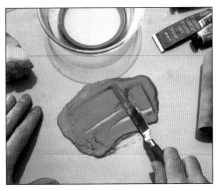

seven *Blend the primary colours (if using) thoroughly on a sheet of glass, using a palette knife.*

eight *Run the paint roller through the ink until it is thoroughly coated.*

nine *Apply an even coating of ink to the potato stamp.*

ten *Lay the prepared fabric on the blanket and print the pattern at random. Re-ink the potato after every two printings to vary the intensity of the colour. Leave the finished fabric to dry, then hem the edges by hand or machine. Make matching napkins the same way.*

NEW WAYS WITH NAPKINS

NAPKINS IN JEWEL-BRIGHT colours add a wonderful and inexpensive splash of brilliance to any dining table and immediately conjure up visions of hotter climates and more exotic places. Choose tapestry wools in strong colours to edge the napkins and trim each one in a different style, adding buttons and beads where appropriate. They will prove really eye-catching used with a plain, boldly coloured tablecloth, country-style china and chunky knives and forks.

YOU WILL NEED
coloured linen napkins
coloured tapestry yarns
tapestry needle
large button
about 50 tiny multicoloured beads
tailor's chalk (optional)

one *If your napkin has an open-work edging, work cross-stitch following the decorative holes in the edge. If not, work evenly spaced cross-stitch along the edge. Attach a button with tapestry yarn at one corner.*

two *Work the edge of the second napkin in blanket-stitch by holding the thread under the needle and pulling the point of the needle through. Take a few strands of tapestry wool, knot them in the centre and stitch them to one corner.*

three *For the bead edging, work out a design by arranging the beads on a flat surface. You could mark these on the napkin first, by chalking tiny dots where you feel the beads should be. Sew the beads securely in place.*

four *Complete the edging with running stitch. Simply take the thread and weave it in and out of the fabric at regular intervals, to form a pretty line of stitches about 1cm (½in) from the edge.*

CROSS-STITCH NAPKIN

SUCCESSFUL CROSS-STITCH relies on the stitches being regular, so checked or gingham fabric provides an ideal ready-made grid. This very easy project is an ideal place to start if you have not done much embroidery before. The cotton fabric should be quite thick and coarsely woven, with a thick embroidery thread to match. Cross-stitch will also add a handmade quality to a set of bought table napkins.

YOU WILL NEED

1m (1yd) heavyweight checked cotton fabric

dressmaker's scissors

dressmaker's pins

needle and tacking (basting) thread

sewing machine and matching sewing thread

embroidery scissors

stranded embroidery floss, in bright contrast colour

embroidery needle

one *Cut the fabric into four rectangles 35cm x 48cm (14in x 19in). Turn under the raw edge on each side, then fold over again to make a narrow hem. Pin and tack (baste).*

two *Machine-stitch with matching thread, using straight or zigzag stitch.*

three *Cut a length of embroidery floss double the width of the first napkin. Thread the embroidery needle, using all six strands, and knot the end. Leaving a blank row of checks, start at one end of a row of checks, with the knot on the reverse side. Make diagonal stitches across alternate squares to the end of the row. Finish with a neat double stitch.*

four *Re-thread the needle as before. Work back along the same row, crossing over each diagonal stitch. Repeat to give a pattern of three cross-stitch rows at both ends of each napkin.*

TEMPLATES

Trompe l'oeil linoleum page 36

Country-style shelf page 66

Vermeer-style marble page 38

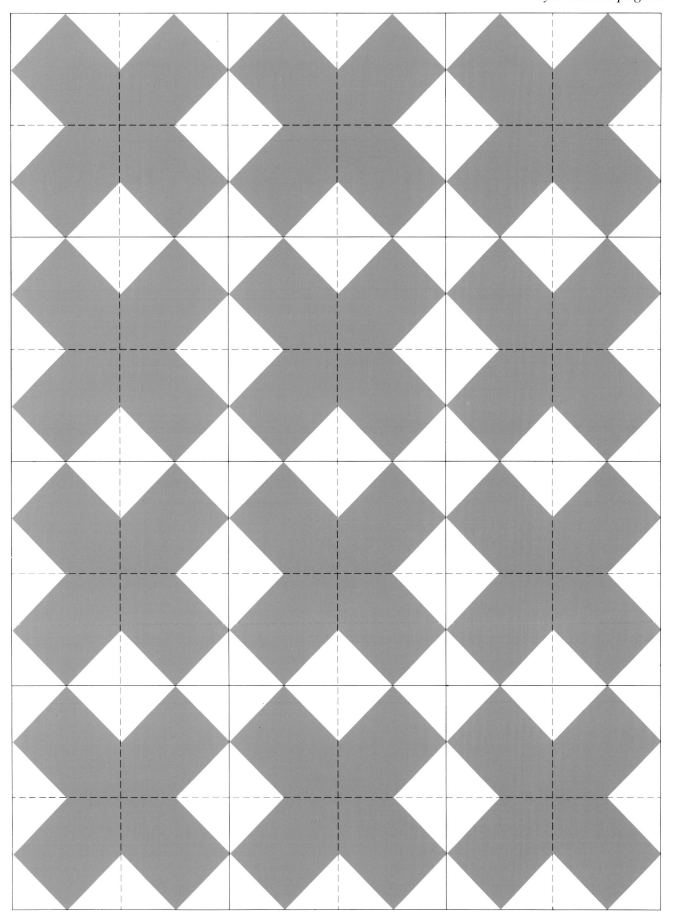

Index

ACKNOWLEDGEMENTS
The publishers would like to
thank the following for
creating additional projects
in this book:
Judy Smith: Cut-above Tiles
pp 24–5; Painted "Brick"
Tiles pp 26–7; Tuscan
Doorway pp 28–31; Punched-
tin Wall pp 32–33.
Catherine Tully: Trompe
l'oeil Linoleum pp 36–7;
Vermeer-style Marble
pp 38–41; Sheet-metal Tread
Mats pp 42–3; Stencilled
Hardboard pp 44–7.
Andrea Spencer: On the Shelf
pp 70–1; Tactile Tablecloth
pp 84–5; New Ways with
Napkins pp 90–1.

ADDITIONAL PHOTOGRAPHY
Tim Imrie: p 11 bottom left.
Spike Powell: p 8 top left; p
10 bottom right. Adrian
Taylor: p 9 top right. Peter
Williams: p 13 bottom left.
Polly Wreford: p 12 top right,
p 13 top right.